GOD GIVE ME PEACE

CHARLES R. JARVIS

GOD GIVE ME PEACE

To arrange for discounted copies for churches, book stores and libraries, please contact the publisher at:

Box2GSM@gmail.com

Printed in the U.S.A.

CONTENTS

I dedicate this book to my Lord and Savior Jesus Christ — The Prince of Peace and the author of peace beyond understanding.

And to my wife Brenda who has brought so much peace to my life.

INTRODUCTION

War and Peace is a 1,455-page book by Russian Author Leo Tolstoy. It is set during the Napoleonic Wars and takes an average reader at least 10 days to read. It is considered a classic of world literature. *This Little Book* is nothing like War and Peace. *God Give Me Peace* is about the inner peace that we all seek in this unsettled world in which we live.

Oh, for a peaceful world. But that's not in anyone's believable prophesy. The first recorded war began around 1300 B.C., one of the Trojan Wars. Here 3,300 years later the world is full of war. Since the turn of the 21st

Century (2000) there have been about 130 conflicts that can be considered war. People killing people.

"We're not going to have peace — permanent peace — until the Prince of Peace comes," evangelist Billy Graham wrote in his book, *Peace With God.* Obviously he was referring to the return of Jesus Christ.

The subject of this book is the peace that God offers us today. The quest for this peace is not negotiated for, nor does it come when one country or faction is overwhelmed and must lay down its arms. The quest for this peace is a personal battle that is won when the combatant surrenders to the all-knowing, all-powerful and ever-present God Almighty.

This Little Book will explore what real personal peace is: where it can be found, how it can be achieved and how one's life benefits from its acquisition. So, a prayer we all should pray is, "God, give me peace."

CHAPTER 1

FIND A
PEACEFUL
PLACE

Dictionary.com gives pretty short shrift to the meaning of peace. It primarily relates it to the absence of war. But Webster's Dictionary of 1828 relates it more personally. It says peace, in a general sense, is a state of quiet or tranquility; freedom from disturbance or agitation; applicable to society, to individuals, or to the temper of the mind.

We as humans thrive in peaceful settings, places of serenity and calmness. We breathe easier and our contentment level is much higher. Such places promote agreement and encourage meditation on the good things in our lives. Everyone needs such a place for a retreat from the voluminous catalog of disruptions to one's peace in the world today.

We have lived the city life. I have lived in Charleston, West Virginia; Charlotte and Raleigh, North Carolina and my wife, Brenda spent more than 17 years in what was, at that time, the world's largest city, Mexico City, where she resided with 30 million people. Traffic noise, emergency sirens, the roar of aircraft overhead and all manner of racket generated by so many people so confined made for a continuous bothersome din. In cities, only the best insulated homes can totally quiet the barrage of noise.

We now are blessed to have two small residences located in rural settings, away from the maddening crowds. One of our homes is a pre-Civil War house situated on five acres of perfectly flat ground. It is surrounded by hundreds of acres of farmland and the neighbors are not close by. Our winter home is in south Georgia's coastal region. Our house is a small cottage with two-and-half acres of ground. Both places have a quiet feeling. When our friends visit us they often comment about how peaceful our places are. We have made a conscious effort to pray over both homes that they would be places of peace and tranquility. God has answered those petitions.

We certainly feel at peace in both locations. Our old farmhouse is more than 170 years old. It's a solid old place with large hand hewn beams supporting the structure. Yes, it has settled some over the years, so some of the floors are not very level. An amazing feature of the house is that it was so situated, in relationship to the sun, that awnings on the south-side windows provide natural air conditioning for the house. On the hottest days of an Ohio summer, sometimes in the low 90-degree level, the house is comfortably cool if we keep the doors and windows closed. Overhead fans keep us comfortable on the warmest nights.

When weather forecasters strike fear with storm warnings including high winds, the old house provides us peace of mind. It has withstood hundreds of episodes of high velocity winds over its long existence. I suppose a direct hit by a powerful tornado would cause significant damage, but God has protected it from that, so far.

This house provides us with two porches where we love to sit. The back porch has a perfect view of the morning sunrise where we can eat breakfast and watch the wonder of a new day being born. It has offered us many opportunities to photograph a spectacular sunrise and we have take advantage of a lot of them. The front porch faces directly west, so in the evenings we sit and marvel at God's artwork in the sky as the sun goes down. What a peaceful way to start and end the day.

In Georgia, our property has a mixture of tall, majestically-straight hardwood trees and short and tall palm trees. There is just something about a palm tree that gives peace to my heart. The azaleas herald in the springtime and the flowering bulbs reappear giving splashes of vibrant colors to brighten the sunny days even more. We are blessed with two peaceful retreats.

You probably are searching for more peace in your life or you wouldn't have picked up *This Little Book*. If so, one of the key things you need is a peaceful place. Hopefully there is some little niche in your residence where you can find some peace and quiet. If the kids are always bouncing off the walls and demanding your attention, maybe not. It could be, if your energy level allows, you need to stay up later or get up earlier to find that quiet time. But a quiet time in a peaceful place is a good starting point to get more peace in your life.

Unfortunately, peace is not a constant state. Some people have it most of the time, and that's what we are aiming for here. Some people have it frequently and others have it, but have it rarely, and some folks are in a constant stage of agitation and don't know how to break the cycle. If you think you are at a low level on the peace scale, finding a peaceful place to meditate and consider and plan your life is a great beginning.

Take a minute and think about the most peaceful place you have experienced in your lifetime.

For me, I think it was when I was 13 years old. I had ridden a Greyhound bus, by myself, without adult supervision, from Charleston, West Virginia, to Oceanside, California, where my sister was living. She had two small children who needed a babysitter for the summer, so she paid for me to go out to do that job. While I was there, she and her husband took me and the kids on a weekend camping trip to Mount Palo Alto. I had learned in grade school about the astrological research observatory on Mount Palo Alto. It had a large telescope to study the stars and planets and was located there because of the normally clear sky conditions. We camped out on the hillside and slept in the open in sleeping bags. When darkness came, I was lying there staring up at the stars. I was, I guess you could say, star-struck. The stars were huge and the sky was so black the brightness of the stars seemed magnified. It was as if I was lying among the stars and it seemed as though I could reach up and touch them. It was beautiful and the quietness of that space was so peaceful. I was at peace and full of God's wonder.

> *When I look at your heavens,*
> *(I see) the work of your fingers,*
> *the moon and the stars,*
> *which you have set in place*

Psalms 8:3 ESV

I have experienced many peaceful places. Some church sanctuaries have a magnificent peacefulness. Sitting alone in a sanctuary will give you the sense the presence of God; after all, any church is considered God's house. Your thoughts will likely go to the people who have been in those pews before you. You might consider the earnest prayers for help that have been lifted up to God from that place. Or you might ponder the lives that have been changed there by the acceptance of Jesus Christ as savior.

I watched the sun come up from a mountainside in West Virginia one fall morning and enjoyed the scene of a farmer bring his cattle herd in from their summer pasture. The morning fog was lifting and the quiet on that mountain top was so peaceful. In my younger days a horseback ride through the woods and along back roads in West Virginia was wonderfully peaceful. Fall walks in a forest are a peaceful time and place. Watching a sunrise or sunset at the beach, is serene. Sitting in the shade by a babbling stream is so soothing.

He maketh me to lie down in green pastures:
he leadeth me beside the still waters.

Psalms 23:2

Take a minute and let your mind take you back to a time where you really felt at peace, a peace so powerful it shut out the clamor of the world and loosened the grip of your worries. Find a place like that again.

Chapter 2

Disrupters of Peace

O ur world in this 21st Century is full of disruptions to our lives. A disruption is a forcible separation or division of something. It's the cause of an interruption in the normal flow of things. If a person or entity causes a disruption in a due course, that person or entity becomes a disrupter.

The arrival of the pilgrims on North America's soil disrupted the control of the land by the Native Americans. The American Revolution disrupted the British Empire's design for the new colonies in America. The automobile disrupted the horse-and-buggy culture. The computer disrupted and greatly increased the speed of countless processes that had before been done by hand or human calculation. The internet disrupted how mail is delivered, news is communicated and products are sold.

Peace on American soil was abruptly disrupted by the December 7, 1941 attack by the Japanese on Pearl Harbor and on September 11, 2001, when terrorists flew jet liners filled with innocent passengers into the World Trade Center towers in New York City, the Pentagon in Washington, D.C., and the ground in Stoystown, Pennsylvania.

The Covid 19 pandemic disrupted all aspects of life all around the world in 2020 and 2021.

We individuals are affected by worldly disruptions such as those listed above. Our peace of mind is further disrupted by disrupters rooted within ourselves. Worry, bitterness, jealousy, coveting and being unforgiving are disrupters of our inner peace.

Many of us are likely to be afflicted by more than one, if not all, of these disrupters of peace.

You can't have real peace with worry. Worry is like riding a roller coaster. It takes you up and down, turns you upside down and brings you back to the very place your started with nothing accomplished.

Roughly 85 percent of the things people worry about never happen, according to a study by Cornell University. That study further discredited worry as it found that of the 15 percent of the worries that did happen, 79 percent of the time the outcome of those worries was better than expected, or the worrier had learned something useful from the experience.

A friend of mine once said, "The stuff your worry about rarely happens, it's the stuff you never think about that gets you."

According to a report by the Baton Rouge Clinic, a member of the Mayo Clinic Care Network, worry can be detrimental to your health.[1] Worry leads to anxiety and extended periods of anxiety can lead to major health issues. Worry may cause the following symptoms:

- You may feel restless, edgy or jumpy

- You may feel tired and have no energy

- You may find it difficult to concentrate or be distracted

- You may have difficulty sleeping

- You may feel anxious or have a panic attack

- You may have aches and pains due to muscle tension

- You may have physical symptoms, like headaches or stomach aches

- You may turn to unhealthy behaviors, like overeating, drinking alcohol or taking drugs

I believe the most dangerous time for worry is when you are battling a serious health issue. If your worry causes any of the above symptoms while your body is trying to heal or ward off injury or illness, especially during cancer treatments, worry will only complicate the healing. Positive thoughts will be much more beneficial to your situation.

Worry does not empty tomorrow of its sorrow.
It empties today of its strength.
Corrie Ten Boom

The futility of worry and the detrimental health effects implore us to avoid worrying, but it's unlikely you can do that "cold turkey". There is a mountain of advice online about how to curtail your worrying, but the quickest and surest way to step away from worrying is by trusting God more. We will get into that in the next chapter.

Follow peace with all men, and holiness, without which no man shall see the Lord: Looking diligently lest any man fail of the grace of God; lest any root of bitterness springing up trouble you, and thereby many be defiled.
Hebrews 12:14-15 KJV

One of the greatest disrupters of our peace of mind is bitterness. I have seen people completely consumed by bitterness. Bitterness can be born of many things but it generally is the result of its victim feeling mistreated by someone or some circumstance. Men and women can be bitter over divorce. Divorced women can be bitter over being forsaken by a husband who chose another woman over her. Or the settlement of the marriage's assets may not have been seen as fair, and these situations in reverse can affect men as well.

I believe I watched a friend die from bitterness after his divorce settlement left him with a very large spousal support payment each month. My friend was a frugal guy and he was meticulous about his appearance, his home and his vehicles. I don't know the circumstances surrounding his divorce, but I'm sure he felt it was not his fault. He was ordered to pay thousands per month in spousal support. I know he did so grudgingly and I watched him as his health deteriorated and heart problems led to his death. He had expressed his bitterness to some of his friends.

*Holding a grudge is like drinking poison
and waiting for the other person to die.*
Emmet Fox

Bitterness can spring from the next three conditions in my list of disrupters of our inner peace — jealousy, coveting and being unforgiving. Jealousy and coveting are often intertwined. Two much attention to, and desire for, worldly goods can give rise to jealousy. Jealousy is dangerous to our relationships.

Mindfulhealthsolutions.com says "jealousy is often rooted in insecurities and fears that a person may not even realize they have. These could include fear of oversimplification, fear of inadequacy, fear of abandonment, fear of being replaced, and fear of being judged." [2]

Jealous thoughts can be real, of course, but often they are imagined threats to our relationships. Most often our jealous thoughts erupt from our own insecurities listed above. A critical element of any relationship is trust. A lack of trust can foster the development of jealousy. Jealousy has been the cause of murder since Cain slew Abel (Genesis 4:8). Extreme jealousy in a relationship is toxic at best and fatal at worst.

Jealousy in romance is like salt in food—A little can enhance the savor, but too much can spoil the pleasure and, under certain circumstances, can be life-threatening.

Maya Angelou

Coveting is a strong desire for something you don't have. It usually pertains to worldly goods that someone else has or can afford. Desiring things that are good for you, such as our quest for more inner peace, would not be considered coveting.

Take care, and be on your guard
against all covetousness,
for one's life does not consist in the abundance
of his possessions.

Luke 12:15 ESV

Being unforgiving is a weight too heavy to bear. It will do your heart more damage than you know. It will steal your happiness. It will damage your relationships and if you are a child of God, it will quell your relationship with the Holy Spirit that indwells you.

Forgiveness takes many forms, but generally, it involves a decision to let go of resentment and anger. Forgiveness is such a key component to finding peace that it will be dealt with more deeply in the next chapter.

So, to prepare our hearts for peace, we must be determined to rid our hearts and minds of worry, bitterness, jealousy, coveting and unforgiving. As David penned one of his many Psalms he asked God this:

Search me, O God, and know my heart:
try me, and know my thoughts:
And see if there be any
wicked way in me, and lead me
in the way everlasting.

Psalm 139:23-24

Chapter 3

Forgiving Means Forgetting

On a hill called Calvary, just outside of Jerusalem, Jesus Christ was nailed to two beams which we have come to know as the cross. He had been severely beaten by Roman soldiers, who showed no mercy. Who can imagine the agony he experienced in those hours before his death?

Then Jesus said, Father, forgive them;
for they know not what they do.

Luke 23:34 KJV

Could any among us do that. It would certainly be unlikely.

Fast forward to the year 1981, when this story unfolded: Pope John Paul II, one of the most beloved popes in the Catholic Church's history, was shot by a 23-year old man from Turkey who had been radicalized by a terrorist group. His name was Ali Agca, according to the *Vatican News*. The Pope was seriously wounded and it took surgeons five hours to bring him to a stable condition.

The Vatican reported that the Pope, while on his way to the hospital, committed himself to forgive his assailant. After Agca was tried and sentenced, Pope John Paul went to the prison and met face-to-face with the young man and pronounced his forgiveness.

"We met as fellow human beings and as brothers," Pope John Paul said after the meeting.[1]

There are many, many stories published in newspapers and books of examples of forgiveness that would test any of us if we were in the shoes of those who were victims of attempted murder or other serious crimes. Forgiveness by victims and their families of horrific accidents caused by someone's extreme negligence sometimes makes the news because it is such an uncommon occurrence.

But many of us are guilty of letting much less-serious offenses by friends, relatives, acquaintances and even strangers, to cause us to have an unforgiving spirit. Relationships are known to be broken over the slightest of slights.

If we are unforgiving of someone for some transgression, we are carrying a grudge against that person. Many people — famous or common — have said "Life is too short to carry a grudge." Grudges are disrupters of peace and happiness. We can be in the best of moods and in the blink of an eye something brings that grudge back to mind. Our tranquility is shattered. It can take minutes or hours to put the grudge aside once more.

The late Ed Koch, former mayor of New York City, had this view of carrying a grudge:

There's enormous energy required to carry grudges - enormous energy! And I'm getting too old to expend my energy that way, 'cause I think every person has a limited amount of energy. So I have given up all grudges.

Ed Koch

A lack of forgiveness causes grudges. Grudges cause bitterness. Bitterness causes various health concerns and it even can cause your countenance to change. Your countenance, or facial appearance can have a severe effect on how people perceive you and relate to you.

Calvin Coolidge, the 30th president of the United States, was notorious for his less-than-happy countenance. Alice Roosevelt Longworth, an outspoken daughter of the 26th president, Theodore "Teddy" Roosevelt, is credited with saying of Coolidge,"He is a very nice fellow, only he was weaned on a pickle."

Unusual for a politician, Coolidge was rarely photographed wearing a smile. His official White House portrait has him with piercing eyes and a somber countenance.

Historians say Coolidge suffered from depression from childhood. His mother passed when he was 12 and his father was a strict authoritarian. As an adult he suffered from heartburn and indigestion, migraines and chronic insomnia. Any or all of these things could have been the reason for his sad countenance, but there must have been something from his past he could not let go of.

Get rid of all bitterness, rage and anger,
brawling and slander,
along with every form of malice.

Ephesians 4:31 NIV

Bitterness also causes negativity, which can cause people to not want to be around you, because you disrupt their positive thoughts and vibes.

The website *tacomachristiancounseling.com* gives this advice: "The key to fighting bitterness is forgiveness. When you forgive, you let the other person off the hook for their wrongs. You can hand your hurt over to God, who will handle it with perfect justice. Then you can step into freedom instead of being held in the bondage of bitterness."[2]

As children of God, when we ask him to forgive our sins, he does. And, he also forgets them.

For I will be merciful to their unrighteousness,
and their sins and their iniquities
will I remember no more.

Hebrews 8:12 KJV

The writer of Hebrews went on to re-emphasize that God forgives and forgets:

This is the covenant that I will make with them
after those days, saith the Lord, I will put my

laws into their hearts, and in their minds will I write them; And their sins and iniquities will I remember no more.

Hebrews 10:16-17 KJV

God speaks of his forgetting of our sins in this passage:

I am he who blots out your transgressions for my own sake, and I will not remember your sins.

Isaiah 43:25 KJV

Our mission as a Christian is to strive each day to be more righteous, more Christ like. When we accept God's grace, we must also give grace to others. We must forgive *and* forget, as God does.

Have you ever had someone tell you that they forgave you of something, then at a later date they threw it up to you again? Have you ever done that yourself? That is evidence of our hypocrisy in our forgiving.

A friend and coworker of mine had a great deal of wisdom in managing people. Sometimes, when someone breaks a rule or offends us in some way, we tend to just "let it pass." We don't deal with it then and there. It's like we pick up a rock to throw at the offender, but instead of throwing the proverbial stone, we just put it in our pocket. In ensuing days that offender might break a different rule or they may have offended us in a different way. Instead of forgiving them in our heart and mind or dealing with the issue then and there, we again let it pass. We put another stone in our pocket. Similar situations occur as time goes on. Our pocket has become full of rocks and we've finally had enough. So we unload on the offender. We pull out and describe each stone and hurl it at the offender. The relationship has just exploded into a barrage of flying stones.

This story illustrates how we must not only forgive transgressions against us, but how we must forget them.

Without forgiveness of others, there cannot be a predominance of peace in your life.

CHAPTER 4

PEACE COMES FROM SURRENDER

Never, ever give up! Many people with good intentions have imparted that imperative to me many, many times in my lifetime. Set a goal. Put a plan in place to achieve that goal. Devote all the time necessary, work hard and smartly; push on past your normal strength. Don't let obstacles deter your success; if you can't overcome them, work around them. If you need tools and supplies, find a way to acquire them. If you suffer a setback, regroup and take a different path to your goal. You might have to fight your battle more than once to achieve your goal. But, if it is really important to you, never, ever give up!

I lived by this mantra for many years of my life, both as a youth and as an adult. I taught myself several skills and trades. I devoted countless 16-hour days, expended many dollars and volunteered my time in exchange for experience. I was almost singularly focused on the "new thing." That approach served me well in learning how to be a radio announcer, a news reporter, an editor, a publisher, an auctioneer, a gospel songwriter, a singer, a lay speaker and an author.

I tell you all of that to illustrate that none of that works if your goal is inner peace. All of the above mentioned endeavors, as well as my passion for baseball and basketball as a youth, were achieved by relying on my own will. We can't achieve inner peace solely through marshaling our own will.

We must surrender to God's will.

Surrender? Isn't that giving up? Yes it is.

And he said to them all,
If any man will come after me,
let him deny himself, and take up
his cross daily, and follow me.
Luke 9:23 KJV

Jesus asked his chosen disciples to give up their worldly goods and their self will and to follow him. They forsook their vocations, their families, their treasures and they walked with Jesus, fully trusting in him. They surrendered their own will to his.

To fully surrender to God, we have to tackle two major obstacles in our minds.

First, we have to accept that it is God, Jesus and the Holy Spirit — the Holy Trinity — who really are in control of our lives. Each of these are omnipotent, omniscient and omnipresent — all powerful, all knowing and ever present. It is a sweet comfort that we have such knowledge and power controlling our lives.

We can set all the goals we want, make all the plans we want, but we are successful only if it is God's will. By surrendering to God, we allow ourselves access to his guidance, his wisdom and his power, which can be transformational.

Secondly, we must know that God is big enough to handle our biggest concerns, as well as those of everyone else who is tugging at him for attention to their issues.

Our God is big. Really big. He's so big our earthly minds cannot comprehend his vastness.

Great is our Lord, and of great power:
his understanding is infinite.

Psalm 147:5 KJV

Infinite means without limit or boundary. That is big, really big! The Bible tells us he can measure all the waters of earth in the hollow of his hand. He can measure heaven with his span, and he has accomplished many other great feats.

Who has measured the waters in the hollow
of his hand, or with the breadth of his hand
marked off the heavens? Who has held the dust
of the earth in a basket
or weighed the mountains on the scales
and the hills in a balance?

Isaiah 40:12 NIV

Here is an experiment for you. See how much water you can hold in the palm of your hand. Compare that with the water in one lake or one ocean. That gives us a pretty clear picture of how small we are and how big God is. No matter how big we think our problems are, God is big enough to handle them with ease.

When we accept these two precepts, we are on the road to inner peace. Now that we know that God is in charge of all things and he is big enough to handle that job, it is time to start surrendering lots of things to him.

Can you surrender your will, as the Apostles did? Can you confide in God what your plan is and ask him if it is in his will as well? You have been given free will, so you have to choose to let God control your life.

Country music artist Carrie Underwood had a hit song in 2006 entitled "Jesus, Take the Wheel."[1] The song is a story about a young mother, with her child in the back seat, when she loses control of her car on an icy road. As the vehicle is spinning she realizes she is helpless. She surrenders and pleads for Jesus to take the steering wheel. Like most of us, the young mother thought she had everything under control, but when she realized she couldn't calm the situation by her own power, she cried out to Jesus. And when the car came to a safe stop, she accepted Jesus as her Savior.

The song was an award-winner for Underwood and its writers, Brett James, Gordie Sampson and Hillary Lindsey. In 2007 it was the Grammy's song of the year.

The song always reminds me of a bumper sticker that was popular years ago, it read: "Jesus is My Co-Pilot." It wasn't long after that sticker showed up someone came up with a better one: "If Jesus is your Co-Pilot, Change Seats."

Remember, you don't have to wait until you are in the middle of dire circumstances to surrender your will to God's.

Can you surrender your thoughts? We need to let the Holy Spirit fill our minds with God's thoughts. Our earthly minds are so easily swayed to earthly, even sinful, thoughts.

Set your affection on things above,
not on things on the earth.
Colossians 3:2 KJV

Can you surrender your body? Can you surrender your addictions? Can you surrender your anger, wrath, malice, blasphemy, profane and vulgar words? Can you surrender to the truth in all circumstances and situations?

Tossing all of these obstacles to peace into the garbage can at once would be wonderful, but you most likely will have to discard these disrupters of peace one at a time. The goal is to get better each day, striving to the mark of peace and contentment. The more you surrender, the more peace you will have.

I encourage you to choose love over those disrupters.

Therefore, as God's chosen people, holy and dearly loved, clothe yourselves with compassion, kindness, humility, gentleness and patience. Bear with each other and forgive one another if any of you has a grievance against someone.

Forgive as the Lord forgave you. And over all these virtues put on love, which binds them all together in perfect unity.
Let the peace of Christ rule in your hearts, since as members of one body you were called to peace. And be thankful.

Colossians 3:12-15 NIV

CHAPTER 5

FORGIVE YOURSELF

One of the highest barriers to inner peace for some people is the inability to forgive themselves. Many of us are not burdened by such a heavy weight. An inner conflict of blaming ourselves is very foreign to most of us and it is hard to comprehend that some individuals have lived much of their lives being unable to forgive themselves for something that they have done in their past. In many cases, something from their very distant past. They have been living without the comfort of peace, and often with the belief that they could never be "good enough" to accept God's salvation.

I have heard my wife many times tell of her witnessing to women who stop her when she begins to tell them that Jesus can help them change their lives. They often say, "Stop right there. You don't know what I've done." If she gets the chance, she tells them, "It doesn't matter what you've done, it's what Jesus has done for you. He gave his life to pay for your sins."

A clear conscience is necessary to attain a consistent inner peace.

I knew a woman, whom I won't name, who got pregnant in the late 1950s and became an unwed mother. Some in her family made the situation very difficult for her. At the time, pregnancy outside of wedlock was sheer scandal. The combination of condemnation by family and society made it so difficult for her that she carried for decades the belief she was not a good person and she was bound for hell. Toward the end of her life, she was placed in hospice and a relative of her's was compelled to try one more time to get her to understand that she could accept Jesus and spend eternity in heaven.

The relative visited her at her bedside and asked her if she would like to see in heaven her recently departed husband. She immediately said, "But he was a good man." He was a good man, but he had accepted Jesus as his savior and had gone to church by himself for many years. The relative then asked her if she wouldn't like to see her maternal grandmother again, as it was well known that the woman loved her grandmother and held her in very high esteem. She immediately said, "But she was a good woman." She was a good woman who was a Godly example for all of her many children, grandchildren and great-grandchildren.

The relative then explained that being good was not a requirement for getting into heaven. Accepting Jesus as lord and savior was the only requirement. He used the thief on the cross as an example. The woman had been around churches enough as a child, mostly with her grandmother, to know the story of the crucifixion and that there were two thieves crucified with Jesus. He pointed out one thief had recognized that Jesus was the son of God and Jesus told that thief he would be with him in paradise that day.

One of the criminals who hung there hurled insults at him: "Aren't you the Christ? Save yourself and us!"

But the other criminal rebuked him.

"Don't you fear God," he said, "since you are
under the same sentence?
We are punished justly, for we are getting
what our deeds deserve.
But this man has done nothing wrong."

Then he said,

"Jesus, remember me when you come into your
kingdom."

Jesus answered him,

"I tell you the truth,
today you will be with me in paradise."
Luke 23:39-43 NIV

The relative pointed out that the thief had probably lived his entire life as a thief and was not considered in his community to be a good man or a good person. Yet Jesus accepted him and told him he would see him in paradise.

The relative asked the woman if she would like to accept Jesus as her savior and guarantee her eternity in heaven. She said she would like to do that. The relative led her through the prayer of salvation and her decades of torment were put to rest.

Another acquaintance, who obviously has accepted Jesus as her lord and savior, continues to carry guilt or shame that causes her to fret and state clearly that she is "unworthy." Maybe it's something in her past. Maybe it just the fact that, even though she has accepted Jesus as her savior, she still finds sin in her life.

A fact she must not understand is that all of us who have accepted Jesus still have to battle sin and temptation every day. None of us are "worthy," based on how we are able to live our lives. We are only "worthy" because of what Jesus did on the cross nearly two thousand years ago. He paid our sin debt. His payment, paid with his life, covered all of our past, present and future sins.

We all are accosted by sin each day and we have to continually confess them and ask for forgiveness. Not because we could lose our salvation, but to keep a healthy relationship with Jesus and God the Father.

If we confess our sins, he is faithful and just and will forgive us our sins and purify us from all unrighteousness. If we claim we have not sinned, we make him out to be a liar and his word is not in us.

1 John 1:9-10 NIV

This dear lady referenced above seems to be tormented by her perceived "unworthiness." Maybe she is holding herself to a standard that is not attainable. She obviously doesn't understand that God does not want her to suffer such torment. He wants her to accept the free grace that he offers all of us.

Grace and peace be yours in abundance through the knowledge of God and of Jesus our Lord.
Peter 1:2 NIV

For sin shall not have dominion over you: for ye are not under the law, but under grace.
Romans 6:14 KJV

Only as we bow in contrition, confession and repentance at the foot of the cross, can we find forgiveness. There is the grace of God.
Billy Graham

CHAPTER 6

THREE-
MINUTE
SERMONS

C hristianity is blessed with songs and music that praise God the Father, God the Son and the Holy Spirit. Thousands of songs have been written about our Christian faith. No other religion can claim anything close to the catalog of the music of Christianity. While the preaching of God's word is certainly the foundation of Christian worship, the singing of hymns, choruses and songs of praise and worship are just as fundamental in today's churches and religious assemblies. In a service, the music can help establish an attitude of worship. Congregational singing brings the participants together to make a communal joyful noise that honors the deity. It gives us a feeling of togetherness with other Christians. In the "old days," before air conditioning the church windows were open and the Sunday morning hymns became evangelistic outreach to the neighborhood.

Early in my adult life, when I was not in church, I rented a basement apartment in Charleston, West Virginia. It was located next door to a large church. I was serenaded on Sunday mornings by the congregational hymns. It didn't offend me and it seemed to offer a peaceful respite to begin my day off. My landlord, who also was my boss, was a

Christian man and I respected him greatly. He had other apartments to rent, but he probably knew I needed those Sunday morning songs, which I certainly did, as I look back on those days.

We are commanded in the scriptures to sing:

And be not drunk with wine, wherein is excess;
but be filled with the Spirit.
Speaking to yourselves in psalms
and hymns and spiritual songs,
singing and making melody
in your heart to the Lord.

Ephesians 5:18-19 KJV

Christian music, for many people, is a great source of inner peace. I have found that the old hymns and southern gospel songs help me when I am alone, driving or otherwise, to keep my mind on good things. I listen to Christian music, sometimes singing along, and that blocks out the disrupters of peace that want to control my mind.

The old hymns and southern gospel songs have been referred to as three-minute sermons. There is a real message in every one of them. Most were inspired in some way by a particular passage of scripture or the general message of a particular section of God's word.

In the previous chapter I toiled several hours over a number of days pulling together my thoughts on how we have to surrender certain things in our life to Jesus as we seek to acquire a more peaceful life.

There is an old hymn that covers the subject very well in five short stanzas and a chorus. If you have been in a church any number of times, you most likely are familiar with this song written and published in 1896.

I Surrender All

All to Jesus I surrender,
All to him I freely give;
I will ever love and trust him,
In his presence daily live.

Refrain:
I surrender all,
I surrender all,
All to thee, my blessed Savior,
I surrender all.

All to Jesus I surrender,
Humbly at his feet I bow,
Worldly pleasures all forsaken,
Take me, Jesus, take me now.
(Refrain)

All to Jesus I surrender;
Make me, Savior, wholly thine;
Let me feel the Holy Spirit,

Truly know that thou art mine.
(Refrain)

All to Jesus I surrender,
Lord, I give myself to thee,
Fill me with thy love and power,
Let thy blessing fall on me.
(Refrain)

All to Jesus I surrender;
Now I feel the sacred flame.
Oh, the joy of full salvation!
Glory, glory, to his name!
(Refrain)

This song is considered by some to be one of the three most used songs for a church "alter call." An "alter call" is when a pastor or preacher invites anyone in the service to come to the alter to kneel and offer themselves or their burdens to Jesus Christ. Generally the pianist or organist will play the song during this time of reflection. Often the congregation will sing the lyrics providing a near constant reminder for those in attendance and at the alter to "surrender all."

The lyrics were written by Judson Wheeler Van DeVenter, who said the words came to him as he surrendered to the ministry, giving up his teaching career and life-long dream to be an outstanding and famous artist. Mr. Van DeVenter, who went on to become an hymnologist and study and teach the history of hymns, says the words to the song came to him after a five-year struggle to resist the call to ministerial service. Mr. Van DeVenter said he was attending a revival at a Methodist Church in Dundee, Michigan, where he was a member and assisting with the revival meetings, when people began encouraging him to become an evangelist. Five years later, he decided to "surrender all" of his former hopes and dreams to become an evangelist.

Soon after his surrender, Mr. Van DeVenter was at the East Palestine, Ohio, home of George Sebring, founder of the Sebring Camp Meeting and Bible Conference, when words to the song came to him. His friend Winfield S. Weeden put music to the lyrics, and a great hymn of the faith was born.

Van DeVenter went on to be a professor of hymnology at the Florida Bible Institute where he met a young man who would go on to be a legendary evangelist, Billy Graham. Graham used "I Surrender All" regularly at his Crusade meetings.

Mr. Van DeVenter passed away in 1939 at age 43.

Many modern singers have recorded this old hymn, including Mahalia Jackson, Aundrae Crouch, Little Richard, Glen Campbell, Cece

Winans, Amy Grant, the Newsboys and Carrie Underwood.

Wikipedia.com[1] has an extensive section about the song, including a story about how Oprah Winfrey says "I Surrender All" has played a pivotal role in her life. Before her mega stardom, while she was still hosting a local show on a Chicago station, Oprah auditioned for the role of Sophia in the 1985 film *The Color Purple.* She desperately wanted the role but she was told that "real" actresses were being considered for the role. Oprah, in a final attempt to be considered, went to a weight-loss camp. During her trying workouts, running on a track, she said she surrendered her desperate desire to God and sang "I Surrender All" until it brought her a sense of peace and release. After a workout she received a call from Steven Spielberg offering her the part. For her performance she was nominated for an Academy Award and a Golden Globe.

Later that year her television show went national, solidifying her iconic career.

Much comfort and peace is available through hymns, gospel music and praise and worship songs.

CHAPTER 7

FIND TIME
FOR PEACE

C locks have changed significantly over the past 50 years. We have gone from wind-up clocks to atomic clocks; electric clocks to battery-powered clocks. Clocks with two or three "hands" pointing to standard numbers or Roman numerals have transitioned to digital readouts that give you the precise time without the need for any mental calculations. But no matter how they are powered or how you read them, they all still do pretty much the same thing — they tell us what time it is.

Knowing what time it is has never been more important, as our lightning-fast-paced lives require synchronization.

Albert Einstein, widely known as one of the greatest and most respected scientists of all time, said time really only has one purpose — to keep everything from happening at once. The collision course of responsibilities and events that our daily lives endure can cause a severe lack of peace, if not properly scheduled. The pressure of having too much to do and not enough time to do it is unsettling and tiresome. If you see a never-ending cycle of days filled with too much to do and too little time, the peaceful life we seek will seem unobtainable. Our lives are broken down into finite periods of 24 hours per day, and if we don't control our days, our days will control us, robbing us of our hope for a peaceful existence. That ever-spinning merry-go-round will just leave us dizzy, disheartened and dreadfully discouraged.

Some of us need to seriously consider improving the scheduling and management of our time. A poll in 2015 found that 48 percent of Americans, about 150 million people, felt they had too little time to accomplish all they had to do. I can't imagine that that percentage hasn't grown in the ensuing years. Scientists have not found a way to make more time, so we've got to make some critical decisions, if we want to turn our chaotic life into a more peaceful one.

A good idea would be to start by analyzing our days. How are we spending our days? What events, tasks or work are consuming significant amounts of a day?

Let's separate our tasks or events into three buckets.

- Things we have to do

- Things we ought to do

- Things we want to do

Do this for each day of the week. First, put the "have to do" things in the time slots when they have to be or can be done. If there is some flexibility when they can be scheduled, use your judgement on what would work best on a given day. When can you easily multi-task? Schedule a specific time for meals, prep time, clean-up time. Is there help available – spouse or children? If so don't be afraid to include them. Set a day for grocery shopping and do it efficiently. Stopping at the store every day is not very efficient. Remember, we are looking for time savings since we can't make more time. If you haven't tuned into ordering your food and supplies online from your grocer, you should. Make your list, order, schedule a time to pick it up and you have saved some real time. It also can save some real money at the same time by limiting impulse buying. You can also save some time by cooking meals in advance, say one evening or on the weekend, freeze them and just heat them up before serving. Set your schedule and deviate from it only in emergency situations.

It seems that men's lives are much more delineated than women's. Women, especially mothers who take seriously their responsibilities for their families, can easily fall into less peaceful lives. Men generally feel responsible for providing for their families and that can get stressful as well. A stressful life is not a peaceful life.

Husbands and wives should work together on their schedules to make them more conducive to peace than stress. And you need to carve out at least a few hours on Sunday. First to attend church. Joining in worship is a peaceful respite. Also, remember, Sunday should be a day of rest with only "have tos" on the agenda.

These are just some quick suggestions, but it's going to take some serious consideration if you are going to get your helter-skelter life into some semblance of order. There are several highly recommended apps available to help organize your daily tasks and events.

People often complain about lack of time, but lack of direction is the real problem.
Zig Ziglar

In Chapter 1 we discussed finding our place of peace. You have to find time to go there and it has to be a priority.

Once you have the things you have to do plugged into your schedule, then we have to start setting priorities. Taking a peaceful break for quiet contemplation is a good place to start for setting your priorities. Sometimes the things we ought to do pile up really fast and we think we have to whittle them down quickly. If there are ten things on that "Ought To Do" list, choose one or two for tomorrow, not all ten. Always try to work in one or two from the "Want To Do" list each day. Accomplishing those should give you a measure of peace and satisfaction and add to the peace and satisfaction of accomplishing the items you check off of the "Have To Do" list.

Always find time for things that give you peace. It has been tried many times and many times it is true that our peace can be improved by doing something beneficial for someone else.

The greatest gift you could give someone
is your time because when you give your time
you are giving a portion of your life
that you will never get back.
Anonymous

Do your little bit of good where you are;
it's those little bits of good put together
that overwhelm the world.

Desmond Tutu

The time you give to someone else really speaks to how much that someone means to you. It buoys their self-worth. Sometimes, however, we let the number of people we should be spending time with add to our frustrations. We need to be at peace with doing what is possible and practical and prioritize how much time we can give away to someone else.

We should consider the "Starfish Story." The late author Loren Eiseley wrote an essay, which has become known as the "Starfish Story" in his book *The Unexpected Universe* published in 1969. The story tells of a boy walking a beach where hundreds of starfish had washed ashore. He was picking them up and throwing them back into the surf. An old man came by and asked him what he was doing. The boy said he was throwing the starfish back into the water so they wouldn't die. The old man said, because there were so many starfish, the boy couldn't possibly throw them all back. He told the boy he couldn't throw enough back to make a difference. The boy picked up another starfish and heaved it back into the sea and said, "I made a difference for that one."

There's only one thing more precious than our time, and that's who we spend it on.

Leo Christopher

Possibly you are someone known for freely giving of your time, and that has resulted in too many people clamoring for your attention. There will come a time, and maybe it has already come, when the demands for your time are over burdensome. That is when it is time to learn to say "No."

Time is the coin of your life. It is the only coin you have, and only you can determine how it will be spent. Be careful lest you let other people spend it for you.

Carl Sandburg

I know people who would rather choke than to say "No" or "I can't do that" to someone. And some of those people (and you know who you are) are at peace with their lives. They do what they can and view it as a ministry of helping. Their family members are at peace with it as well because they know that their loved one thrives on being helpful.

Time is the most valuable thing a man can spend.

Theophrastus

I would be remiss not to caution you about making plans without asking if your plans are in God's will. We should always recognize that God is in charge. We can plan for tomorrow, but God may have other plans. There can be real peace in accepting that.

> *Whereas ye know not what*
> *shall be on the morrow*
> *For what is your life? It is even a vapour*
> *that appeareth for a little time,*
> *and then vanisheth away.*
> **James 4:14 KJV**

Referring to our life on earth as a vapor is James' way of saying it is short in relationship to our eternal life. We have a finite time in our life, but we don't know what that span entails. We desire to live it in peace and we have to make choices to accomplish that end.

Remember this:

> *It's just a matter of time*
> *until time doesn't matter.*

CHAPTER 8

PEACE IS IN JESUS

Repetition is a wonderful tool.

Repetition is a wonderful tool.

Repetition is a wonderful tool.

Get it? Repetition is a wonderful tool! That's why the scriptures, the word of God, repeatedly contain these two words: "Fear not."

There is great debate about how many times "Fear not" appears in the Bible. Preachers often reference that "Fear not" appears 365 times, one for each day. That may or may not be an exaggeration. Some say its more like 100 times. Yet another who said he made a count of that phrase contends it appears a little over 200 times.

No matter what the real number is, "Fear not" is repeated many times in God's word. But when God says it, don't you think once should be enough?

Repetition is a wonderful tool.

Living in fear is not a peaceful life.

Rabbits live in constant fear, especially in the wild. They have an innate fear of humans or larger animals who might be considering them for dinner. Rabbits sleep primarily during the day. They are most active at dawn or dusk. After dark they are on high alert, watchful for would-be predators. Rabbits, tame and wild, will frequently shake in fear. God doesn't want that for us. Such unrest robs us of the peace God prefers for us. Living in fear is also very unhealthful.

Do not be anxious about anything,
but in everything by prayer
and petition, with thanksgiving,
present your request to God.
And the peace of God,
which transcends all understanding,
will guard your hearts
and your minds in Christ Jesus.

Philippians 4:6-7 KJV

The first order of living a life full of peace is the acceptance of Jesus Christ as your Lord and Savior. If you are a child of God, one who has been reborn by faith in Jesus, you are a follower of the author of peace.

Therefore being justified by faith, we have peace with God through our Lord Jesus Christ.
Romans 5:1 KJV

Phil Robertson, patriarch of the Robertson family of Duck Dynasty fame, minces no words when he talks about peace of mind. Speaking at the Gateway Church[1] in South Lake, Texas, Robertson forcefully declared the following:

"Peace of mind. You are never going to have it without Jesus Christ. Ever!
It ain't going to happen!!"

Robertson, inventor of his world famous duck calls, called peace of mind the "rareist (sic) of commodities." Robertson, when he shares his testimony, spares himself nothing when he describes his sinful life before he accepted Jesus Christ as his lord and savior at age 28. He says he served Satan for 28 years but with his conversion he said he would work for God the rest of his life. Well into his 70s, Phil Robertson is a fearless proponent for God Almighty, as is his entire family.

Deion Sanders, one of the most talented and successful athletes of all time, is also an outspoken believer in the peace found in Jesus Christ. He has been quoted this way:

"I tried everything. Parties, women, buying expensive jewelry... Nothing helped. There was no peace, just emptiness inside. When I found Christ, I found what I had been missing all those years."

As one of the very few athletes to compete at the highest levels in two sports, the National Football League and Major League Baseball, Sanders obviously has had access to all the world offers, but he found his peace in Jesus Christ.

These two successful men are really no different than all of us. It took 36 years for me to get serious about my commitment to Jesus. I spent half of my life being controlled by Satan and the last half living securely in the grace of God. Dedication of my life to Jesus at age 36 began a transformation that has been nothing short of miraculous. I am experiencing peace that would be off the charts on any kind of scale measuring peace and contentment.

Here is a truism:

Know Jesus — Know Peace
No Jesus — No Peace

This unattributed axiom can be adjusted to emphasize some of the attributes of inner peace:

Know Kindness — Know Peace
No Kindness — No Peace

Know Forgiveness — Know Peace
No Forgiveness — No Peace

Know Love — Know Peace
No Love — No Peace

Know Faith — Know Peace
No Faith — No Peace

Jesus wants to be your haven of peace. In the 14th Chapter of John, maybe my favorite chapter of the Bible, Jesus tells us about the peace he gives us.

Peace I leave with you, my peace
I give unto you: not as the world giveth,
give I unto you. Let not your heart be troubled,
neither let it be afraid.

John 14:27 KJV

In this chapter, I really wanted to thoroughly research and eloquently explain how Jesus provides, as the scriptures say, "peace which transcends all understanding." Then I realized how futile it would be for me to try to explain what God says cannot be understood. Obviously there is no hope of me understanding it, so how could I explain it. All I know is that handing your cares to Jesus can result in an inner peace bathed in calmness and serenity such as you have never imagined or experienced. (The following is repeated from above for effect)

Do not be anxious about anything,
but in everything by prayer
and petition, with thanksgiving,
present your requests to God.

And the peace of God,
which transcends all understanding,
will guard your hearts and your minds
in Christ Jesus.

Philippians 4:6-7 KJV

Now may the Lord of peace himself
give you peace at all times
and in every way. The Lord be with all of you.

2 Thessalonians 3:16 NIV

CHAPTER 9

SCRIPTURAL PEACE

Leaning on the powerful word of God is rewarding in so many ways, including its drawing of peace to our hearts. The process of rendering peace from God's word starts with the fundamental understanding that God's word is true and was given to us to direct us to righteousness. The Bible is the inspired word of God. It is a place where we can find an-swers that lead us to understanding in a battle between what is true and the deceptions of the world today. The greatest evangelist of our time, Billy Graham, said "It is man and not the Bible that needs correcting."

There are many benefits to committing to the reading of the Bible daily, other than the obvious instruction from God's word. Committing to time with the scriptures means you have to set the world aside for a short time and quiet your life in a peaceful setting. You will slow your heart rate, lower your blood pressure and communicate with God.

All scripture is God-breathed
and is useful for teaching, rebuking,
correcting and training in righteousness,
so that the servant of God
may be thoroughly equipped
for every good work.
2 Timothy 3:16-17 NIV

Ultimately, peace, happiness and contentment lie in knowing that we are pleasing God.
God's greatest desire, his reason for creating
mankind, is that he would have fellowship
with us. That we would commune with him.

*We proclaim to you what we have seen and
heard, so that you also may have fellowship with
us. And our fellowship is with the Father and
with his Son, Jesus Christ*

1 John 1:3 NIV

Fellowship with God and Jesus is a two-way
conversation. We talk to them through prayer.
They talk to us through scriptures and
through the Holy Spirit who indwells us once
we have accepted Jesus as our lord and savior. The Holy Spirit has the unique ability
to know our thoughts *and* to know God's
thoughts, and he can help us to know when

our thoughts and God's thoughts align. The Holy Spirit also helps us to understand the scriptures.

We should be in constant prayer — constant communication — with God, through Jesus Christ. "God help me," is a brief but powerful prayer when we reach a point where we need something stronger than ourselves to deal with a circumstance in our daily existence. You don't need an alter, a church or even a quiet place to call out to God for help or instruction.

Pray without ceasing. In every thing give thanks: for this is the will of God in Christ Jesus concerning you.

1 Thessalonians 5:17-18

At my age, my hands have lost a lot of their effectiveness. I often struggle with things that never caused the slightest concern when I was younger. Opening a package of crackers can be an ordeal. If I'm trying to get a nut on a small bolt in a tight place, I often have to stop and say, "God help me." It certainly works more often than not. I take a second to calm myself, ask him for his help, and an infusion of patience seems to make the task achievable.

I have watched my wife in her prayers as she goes about her housework. She will stop at any time and take a concern to the throne room of Heaven. She is a great example that you can reach out to communicate with Jesus anytime, anywhere. She says he always answers her call. She never gets a busy signal. She's never been put on hold. Her calls go right through every time.

Call to me and I will answer you
and tell you great and unsearchable things
you do not know.

Jeremiah 33:3-4 NIV

God can hear our prayers and those of everyone at one time. God is big — really big, as we discussed in a previous chapter. Not only does he hear the prayers we say out loud, he also hears our silent prayers, those that go through our minds but not out of our mouths.

Before a word is on my tongue
you, Lord, know it completely.
Psalm 139:4 NIV

Reading the Bible every day can take many forms. Some folks like to follow the trail towards reading the Bible through in a year. There are 1,189 chapters in the Bible, an average of 18 per book. To read the Bible all the way through in 365 days requires reading 3.25 chapters each day. There is a lot of information on the internet about how to read the Bible through in a year.

I believe we can be in God's word every day and profit more if we don't attach ourselves to a goal compelling us to "get through" the Bible in a year. Reading three to four chapters a day is considerable reading and if we set that as a goal in our busy day, it's likely we will just be reading, not understanding what God is saying to us.

Many say it is better to read a short passage each day, maybe even a single verse, then meditate on that verse for several minutes during your devotional time. Then think on it throughout the day, as time permits.

In my work life, I would often have to enter into contracts with persons or companies I was doing business with. Early in my career, I would read through a contract and, when finished, wonder what did all of this really mean. I would defer to a friend and co-worker to give me his opinion on the contract. He would always send it back marked with notes throughout that highlighted sections of the contract that were not favorable to us, or more favorable the the other company than we wanted to accept. I had read the contract, but I clearly had not understood it well enough.

In the business world, you just can't just read a contact. You have to parse it into its separate points. There is a process that is recommended:

1. Read the contract through.

2. Read it more than once.

3. What are the separate parts?

4. Do I understand their meaning.

5. Consider how it all relates to you.

In a contract you must see that it contains what you are in agreement with, and if you are not in agreement, there must be further negotiations before you sign it. While each of the five points above are useful in considering your daily scripture reading, the further fine points of understanding contracts are not applicable to the scriptures. You should find agreement with all scriptures, and we must understand there is no room for negotiations on God's word.

Let's take a brief look on how to meditate on a scripture. We will use one of the passages from earlier in this chapter.

All scripture is God-breathed
and is useful for teaching, rebuking,
correcting and training in righteousness,
so that the servant of God
may be thoroughly equipped
for every good work.
2 Timothy 3:16-17 NIV

You have read it through. Now read it again. Now let's separate it into parts.

A. *All scripture is God-breathed*

It is understood that the 66 books of the Bible were written by many different writers. But all the writers were transcribing God's inspiration. The word inspiration, from the Late Latin *inspīrātiōn- means, literally,* "a breathing in." The scriptures are "God breathed."

B. *Scripture is useful for teaching, rebuking, correcting and training in righteousness*

God gave us his word that has been recorded so it can be used for teaching, pointing out contrary thoughts, correcting transgressions and to train us in righteousness. Righteousness is our goal to do what is right in God's eyes.

C. So *that the servant of God*

Who is the servant of God? Me, you — anyone who is serving or wants to serve God, anyone who is doing God's will.

D. M*ay be thoroughly equipped for every good work.*

The scriptures were given to give us the knowledge and understanding as we do God's work in his kingdom here on earth. They ready us for the task God has for us.

Here, you see, these two verses from 2 Timothy 3 have been parsed into four separate thoughts that we should ponder and meditate on. You can see what you might have missed, if you just read it through and moved on to the rest of the chapter.

Starting or ending your day with just a snippet of quiet scriptural meditation can bring a lot of peace into your day or night.

Oh, how I love your law!
I meditate on it all day long.
Your commands are always with me
and make me wiser than my enemies.
I have more insight than all my teachers,
for I meditate on your statutes.

Psalms 119:97-99 NIV

CHAPTER 10

THE POWER OF PEACE

As we walk through this journey toward our goal of a more peaceful life, are we becoming more meek or more powerful? If we have put off our fits of anger, if we have started to accept the things we cannot change and if we have removed some of our major stressors, then we probably are more meek. That means we are on the right track, for God's word says the meek shall inherit the earth.

But the meek shall inherit the earth; and shall delight themselves in the abundance of peace.
Psalms 37:11 KJV

Becoming more meek is synonymous with becoming more righteous. Jesus repeated the thought of Psalms 37:11 in the New Testament.

Blessed are the meek: for they shall inherit the earth. Blessed are they which do hunger and thirst after righteousness: for they shall be filled. Blessed are the merciful: for they shall obtain mercy. Blessed are the pure in heart: for they shall see God.
Mark 5:5-8 KJV

Being meek is not being weak, but the world would have you to believe that meekness is weakness. Meekness is a powerful force, but it is not a force that explodes, it is a force that exudes. Explosions damage and disrupt everything in sight. Meekness exudes calmness and control. It has been accurately described as strength under control

Explosions don't make things better. Explosive blasts leave everything in shambles and almost never can the scattered pieces be fully reassembled. That's why it is absurd to accept the scientific guess that the earth was the result of a big bang (aka explosion). Our earthly home is an almost perfectly round sphere with a little flatness at each pole, according to the National Aeronautics and Space Administration (NASA). It seems physically impossible for an explosion to result in something perfectly round.

In contradiction, meekness often keeps things just the way they were and in harmony, a consistent, orderly or pleasing arrangement of the parts. No reassembly required.

I have observed people who were not subject to being easily provoked to argument or anger. These people were never overbearing. They were people of meekness, but they were far from weak. They listened attentively to the arguments under discussion. Their opinions were well-reasoned and presented in a non-threatening manner. In turn, their thoughts were well-respected and appreciated. Often the strength of their calm approach carried the day.

The meek are also forgiving and more willing to serve others. These Christ-like attributes serve us well and give us a strong platform of influence that we might not seek, but yet attain.

So, are we becoming more meek or more powerful, as we work toward a more peaceful life? That's the question we asked in the first sentence of this chapter. The answer apparently is "both."

James Allen was a British philosopher and pioneer of self-help writing, such as *This Little Book.* He lived in the late 19th Century and died in 1912 at age 48. He had a good take on the strength of being a person of peace.

The more tranquil a man becomes, the greater is his success, his influence, his power for good. Calmness of mind is one of the beautiful jewels of wisdom.

James Allen

The Allen quote also brings to mind this one:

When things change inside you, things change around you

Unknown

The transition to a peaceful existence is not easy, nor an overnight process. It's not easy to change one's outlook on life. A determined, outspoken and forceful person rarely can transform himself into a thoughtful, considerate, kind and gentle persuader. They can have the best ideas, the best solution to a problem but their brashness, directness and steam-roller approach often turns people off and makes them disregard their ideas. It's not impossible for them to change to a kinder, gentler persona, but it is rare when such a transition occurs.

During my 60 years of work experience, from the 1960s to the 2020s, there was great transition on how employees were handled. In the earlier part of my career, one misstep by an employee could lead to instantly being fired by a supervisor or boss. The overseers could be tyrants and get away with it for years. That started to change in the 1980s as better treatment of employees was demanded and secured. I saw, in my career, a significant shift from intolerant managers having the unilateral power to dismiss employees for any reason to a time when human resource departments set direction on how the firing of employees would have to follow specific steps. The focus shifted from how do we get rid of this employee, to how do we save this employee and make him/her a better, more valuable employee. Some managers were able to adapt to the new culture. Some were not capable and ended up losing their jobs. It is hard to change the spots on a leopard, as they say.

Peace is a daily, a weekly, a monthly process, gradually changing opinions, slowly eroding old barriers, quietly building new structures.
John F. Kennedy

I'm pretty sure President Kennedy was talking about societal or world peace when he was quoted this way. However, his words also would relate to how we must go about securing inner peace. It's a marathon, not a sprint. Incremental improvement is the best we can hope for. But, we have to start the journey with the first step of deciding we want a more peaceful existence and asking God to help us with that process. We have to identify our disrupters of peace and work to eliminate or reduce them.

The life of inner peace, being harmonious and without stress, is the easiest type of existence.

Norman Vincent Peale

Do not let the behavior of others

destroy your inner peace.

Dalai Lama

Nobody can bring you peace but yourself.

Ralph Waldo Emerson

Peace begins with a smile.

Mother Teresa

Jesus didn't leave a material inheritance to his

disciples. All he had when he died was a robe.

But Jesus willed his followers something more

valuable than gold. He willed us his peace.

Billy Graham

CHAPTER 11

THE RESULTS ARE IN

How often do you really feel at peace? What we are striving for is a continual peaceful status that is only interrupted infrequently and is quickly restored to peacefulness.

A Pew Research study[1] conducted in 2014 entitled "Frequency of Feeling Spiritual Peace

and Wellbeing" polled more than 35,000 people in telephone interviews. The polling has
some interesting, but not definitive, conclu-
sions. Here are some of them:

Fifty-nine percent of those 35,000 polled
said they felt spiritual peace at least once a
week, followed by these results:

15% once or twice a month

9% several times a year

16% seldom or never

1% didn't know.

They broke the survey results into several
categories. It found that 75 percent of evan-
gelical protestants felt spiritual peace at least
once a week, Catholics at 57 percent, while
mainline protestants were at 56 percent.

Seventy-six percent of those surveyed who
said they believed in God with absolute certainly said they had spiritual peace at least once
a week.   Add the 14 percent that said they
believed in God with some degree of certainty

and you have 90 percent of those who believed in God saying that they had peaceful time each week. The remaining participants who said they didn't believe in God, didn't know if they believed in God, or were not certain at all that they believed in God made up a total of only 10 percent of the respondents who felt at peace at least once a week.

Seventy-one percent of those who said they prayed at least daily were at spiritual peace at least once a week. A large number, 58 percent of the respondents who said they seldom or never prayed, said they seldom or never felt at peace. That certainly speaks to the need for an active prayer life if we are seeking consistent inner peace.

Half of those polled said they attend religious services at least once a week and claimed to have felt at peace at least once a week. Conversely, 60 percent of the respondents who said they seldom, if ever, attended religious services said they seldom, if ever, felt at peace. This is a good testimonial for church attendance if you are seeking consistent inner peace.

The more education the poll's participants had reflected less time of feelings of peace and well-being. Forty-percent of those with high school or less education felt peaceful and well at least once a week. Thirty-three percent of those with college degrees attained that level peace while only 10 percent of those with post graduate degrees were able to attain feelings of peace and wellness at least once a week.

Fifty-one percent of married people in the polling said they experienced spiritual peace and well-being at least once a week. Only seven percent of those living with a partner had that frequency of peace. Thirteen percent of divorced or separated respondents, eight percent of the widowed and 21 percent of those who were never married claimed peace at least weekly.

Seventy-one percent of the people polled who had no children said they had peaceful feelings at least once a week. On the other hand, only 29 percent of the respondents who had children under the age of 18 had outbreaks of peace once a week. I doubt anyone told them that raising children would be easy.

If you would like further information on this study, it can be found at *pewresearch.com*.

I believe those of you reading this book are looking for many more episodes of peace, bliss and tranquility than just once a week or a few times a month. We should be seeking a high majority of moments of peace which are interrupted infrequently by the disrupters that all of us experience from time to time.

In the months since my retirement, I've enjoyed peace and contentment like I've never experienced before. The pressures of a job that carried a large responsibility day after day are now behind me. Any disrupter of my peace carries so much less of a punch than it did prior to retirement.

I was amazed recently at how I was able to smile, and even laugh, at some of life's calamities that tried to spoil my day. I awoke one day to notice that we had no running water in our home. I had suspected for some time that our water well pump was probably near end of life. It had finally died after about 15 years of good service. I had planned that day to take my 13-year-old pickup truck to my trusted mechanic to fix an oil leak that was just discovered. And the following day my wife and I were planning to travel to the western part of the state of Ohio to pay honor to a dear friend who had passed away. After not being able to get a plumber out to install a new pump until the following day, we decided that since we had no running water my wife should leave on her own to make the trip where she could stay at her brother's home before visiting with the deceased's family. I would stay back, get my truck to the garage and be there for the plumber. On my way to the mechanic's garage, I had to stop for gasoline. When I went to open my truck door, the inside door handle broke off in my hand. The author of lies, deceit and disruption was working very hard to spoil my day. His plan didn't work. God had provided me with enough grace to view these setbacks as just bumps in the road. God's provision for me gave me the resources to deal with the issues and the spirit to not let them take my eyes off of God's goodness.

I have told you these things,
so that in me you may have peace.
In this world you will have trouble.
But take heart! I have overcome the world.
John:16:33 NIV

God, grant me the serenity to accept
the things I cannot change
the courage to change
the things I can, and the wisdom
to know the difference.
Reinhold Niebuhr

CHAPTER 12

PEACEFUL THOUGHTS

F acebook is a wealth of worthless information, but there are nuggets of insight available through that foundation of social media, if you are willing to endure most everything else.

You can learn whether your friends are eating healthful foods or enjoying the tasty side of consumption just by seeing the pictures of what they ordered at their latest restaurant visit.

A lot of times the real meat of one's Facebook post is fleshed out in the comments section where one's friends can post their thoughts about the meme you posted or a happening you shared.

My wife published our favorite wedding picture and announced our most recent wedding anniversary. More than 100 people commented with very wonderful and thoughtful comments. Reading through those was a peaceful and gratifying time for us.

A Facebook page titled Working Women posted a meme that asked an intriguing question:

What makes you feel at peace?

That question generated hundreds of answers. I took the time to categorize the answers in the first couple of hundred responses just to get some idea of what things most frequently brought peace to the respondents.

This, obviously, is not a scientific study, but instructive information can be gleaned from the responses:

Prayer was the most-mentioned thing that brought peace to the respondent. That makes a lot of sense. Finding a quiet place to sit and commune with God is a great way to find moments of peace. And when you are finished praying, that peace can carry over when you get back in the real world. In talking with God, you can give him your concerns and burdens. He wants you to trust in him to resolve your issues. He's very capable. When you give your worries to God, they are in good hands. There were other spiritual responses, like faith, in the presence of the Holy Spirit, doing devotions, at church, relying on God, knowing God is with me, reading the Bible, thanking God for his blessings, secure in my salvation, hearing the word and meditating on God's love. As the survey showed in the previous chapter, people of faith more often feel at peace.

Closely behind prayer, with the second most responses, was family. People said they were at peace when they were with their family. Having family physically with you gives you a sense of peace in knowing they all are safe and there is strength in numbers. Being with their children and grandchildren was also part of the results under the heading of family. Spending time with their mate was noted several times, as was being with a baby. Several people said they were at peace when they were with their pets.

The next largest category was being at peace listening to music. Several genres of music were mentioned, including old hymns and praise and worship music. Secular genres were also included.

Nature had several responses. Watching the sun rise an set brought peace to some. Being close to water at the beach or lake and listening to the rain were often mentioned sources of peace.

Other interesting responses included being alone, silence, remembering a loved one, talking with daddy, doing their hobby, watching TV, cooking, cleaning, financial security, coffee, reading a book, being in bed and sleeping.

One replied when being with good people, while another cautioned staying away from negative people.

You see there are many avenues to periods of personal peace. It is likely that one or more of the categories listed above would fit your time and place of peacefulness. For most people peace is like the sea shore, it ebbs and flows. But for those of us with a solid spiritual foundation, faith that God is always with you and it is he that really is in charge of our lives, we have a more stable inner peace and the disrupters of peace are much less effective against us.

There is peace even in the storm.
Vincent van Gogh

Do not let the behavior of others destroy your inner peace.
Dalai Lama

When you do the right thing,
you get the feeling of peace and serenity associated with it.
Do it again and again.
Roy T. Bennett

If you are depressed, you are living in the past.
If you are anxious, you are living in the future.
If you are at peace,
you are living in the present.
Lao Tzu

If there is righteousness in the heart,
there will be beauty in the character.
If there is beauty in the character,
there will be harmony in the home.
If there is harmony in the home,
there will be order in the nations.
When there is order in the nations,
there will peace in the world."

Confucius

Peace is always beautiful.

Walt Whitman

CHAPTER 13

ETCETERA

As we come to the end of *This Little Book*, I want to leave you, the reader, with final thoughts that provide what I believe are the two wisest things anyone can do in their lifetime, but they also are gateways to inner peace:

No. 1

Accept Jesus Christ as your Lord and Savior. Do you know the precise time when you surrendered your heart to Jesus? (If you know that you have accepted Jesus, you may skip to No. 2.

Accepting Jesus is a simple process. First you have to acknowledge that you are a sinner.

> *For all have sinned and fall short*
> *of the glory of God.*
> Romans 3:23 ESV

You must realize that as a sinful being we will one day die.

For the wages of sin is death, but the free gift of
God is eternal life in Jesus Christ our Lord.
Romans 6:23 ESV

You must believe that Jesus is the Son of God and that he gave his life that you might live.

*I also received: that Christ died for our sins
in accordance with the scriptures, that he was
buried, that he was raised on the third day in
accordance with the scriptures.*
1 Corinthians 15:3-4 ESV

If you believe on these things and pray for Jesus to become your lord and savior, He will accept you as a child of God, forgive you of all of your sins and give you life everlasting. You will have been born again and the Holy Spirit will indwell you.

*Jesus answered, Verily, verily, I say unto thee,
Except a man be born again, he cannot see the
kingdom of God.*
John 3:8 KJV

No. 2

Point others to Jesus.

The fruit of the righteous is a tree of life; and he
that winneth souls is wise.
Proverbs 11:30 KJV

Glory be to God

CITATIONS

Chapter 2

1

https://batonrougeclinic.com/what-happens-when-you-worry-too-much/#:~:text=Chronic%20stress%20has%20been%20shown,suppression%20of%20the%20immune%20systemWhat Happens When Your Worry Too Much, Blog Update, Jan. 24, 2022, The Baton Rouge Clinic AMC, a member of the Mayo Clinic Network

2

https://mindfulhealthsolutions.com/the-deeper-meaning-of-jealousy-a-psychological-ex

ploration/mindfulsolutions.com   Deeper Meaning of Jealousy: A Physological Exploration

Chapter 3

1

https://www.vaticannews.va/en/church/news/2020-04/easter-sunday-reflection-vatican-news010.html1Article:Reflections for Divine Mercy Sunday, by Fr. Antony Kadavil, April 2020, *Vatican News*

2

https://tacomachristiancounseling.com/articles/bible-verses-for-fighting-bitterness#:~:text=As%20stated%20earlier%2C%20bitterness%20can,root%20and%20handle%20anger%20triggersTacoma Christian Counseling article: Bible Verses for Fighting Bitterness, tacomachristiancounseling.com

Chapter 4

1

Jesus, Take the Wheel" is a song written by Brett James, Hillary Lindsey and Gordie Sampson, and recorded by American country music artist Carrie Underwood. It was released on October 18, 2005, as the first single from Underwood's debut album Some Hearts (2005).

Chapter 6

1

https://en.wikipedia.org/wiki/I_Surrender_All#:~:text=Van%20DeVenter%20wavered%20for%20five,of%20noted%20evangelist%20George%20Sebring.

Chapter 7

1

Iseley, **Loren** C.,   1907-1977.   1969. *The **Unexpected Universe**. New York, Harcourt, Brace & World. Chicago

Chapter 8

1

https://www.google.com/search?q=Phil+
Robertson+Gateway+Church&rlz=1C5CH
FA_enUS784US784&oq=Phil+Robertson+
Gateway+Church&aqs=chrome..69i57j0i39
0i512i650l5.9207j0j15&sourceid=chrome&i
e=UTF-8#fpstate=ive&vld=cid:b61fbec0,vid
:eJ3VKL6m5v0,st:0

Chapter 11

1

https://www.pewresearch.org/religion/reli
gious-landscape-study/immigrant-status/thir
d-generation-or-higher/frequency-of-feeling
-spiritual-peace-and-wellbeing/at-least-once-a
-week/Pew Research, Religious Landscape
Study, 2014

CHAPTER 14

ABOUT THE AUTHOR

Charles R. Jarvis began writing for a living at age seventeen when he filled in for the editor of his hometown weekly newspaper in Spencer, W.Va., as the editor was recovering from a heart attack. He went on to study journalism at West Virginia University for two years before accepting a position as sports editor of a daily newspaper. He soon was recruited to write for United Press International. His career included copy editing, writing and photography at newspapers before moving into editor and publisher positions for the last 30 years of his 56-year career. He and his wife Brenda have an active Christian ministry as lay speakers and providers of special music for church services in several states. They have residences in Farmdale, Ohio and Brunswick, Ga.

Previous works:

ISBN 979-8-9888503-0-2

God Give Me Wisdom, And This Little Book, which is the first in a series entitled *And This Little Book* published by Golden Street Ministries, P.O. Box 2, Farmdale, OH 44417.

To arrange for discounted copies for churches, book stores and libraries, please contact the publisher at:

Box2GSM@gmail.com